COLOUR HOUSE

COLOUR HOUSE

Vibrant spaces to brighten your world

Harper *by* Design

Contents

Living in Full Colour	7
The Living Room	9
The Kitchen	61
The Bedroom	93
The Bathroom	131
The Outdoors	167

Living in Full Colour

Calming green, passionate red and mellow yellow ... Many people believe colour has the ability to influence our mood, mindset, health and even our creative prowess. While the scientific jury is out on the efficacy of colour therapy, there's no denying the tremendous impact that colour can have on our homes. Whether it's experiencing a surge of joy when walking into a cute, pastel-hued kitchen or feeling an instant pressure drop when relaxing in a living room filled with warm, woody autumnal tones, colour can influence our psyche.

Just as our ancestors used natural pigments like clay and charcoal to colour their dwellings thousands of years ago, so do we. The only difference is we have many more tools (and colour combinations) at our disposal these days. Now we muse over colour swatches at hardware stores, compare upholstery shades at furniture showrooms and bookmark pages of bespoke tiles on our laptops, all in the hope of creating the perfect colour scheme in our home.

From kitschy bedrooms that turn the colour dial up to 10, to outdoor living spaces that take a risk with vivid feature walls, there are countless ways to play with colour in your home. The key to creating your ultimate colour house? Don't be afraid to experiment – life is best lived in full colour.

The Living Room

The scene of late-afternoon naps on the couch, games nights, movie marathons and after-dark tipples with friends, the living room could just be the most important area of any home. The perfect blank canvas on which to express your unique self, your living room is ripe for a colour makeover. Whether you want to showcase an eclectic range of inspirations and influences via vintage prints, floral wallpaper and textured rugs in bright hues, or create an understated, minimalist vibe with muted cool tones, there are no rights or wrongs when it comes to building your dream living room colour scheme. One of the best aspects of the living room is its size – it is generally a large space to play with. Adding colour can be as easy as installing new curtains or investing in cushions and throw rugs. Since living rooms are for living, why not live your best life and embrace the full spectrum of colours when crafting this comfy space?

Colour can be used in different ways for varying effects. A hot-pink wall (left) commands attention, while watermelon couches (above) add subtle pops of colour to the room.

12

The Living Room

The striking fuchsia of this couch is echoed by the cushions' pink highlights, creating harmony in an eclectic room.

Strawberry milkshake tones featured in artwork and soft furnishings are a subdued way to introduce pink to your living room palette.

This candy-pink wall complemented by retro-style tiles with pale pink tones makes for a unique and memorable entryway to a quirky living room.

This sofa, upholstered in a velvety shade of Turkish delight, adds a touch of sweetness to a bare white room (above). If a statement couch feels like a big commitment, try dipping a toe in the water with a few cushions in a similar fabric or a feature wall in the same shade (right).

Mellow tones of peach and spearmint conjure an air of luxe nostalgia.

21

The Living Room

Adding a variety of colours in softer tones creates a sense of lightness and fun without overpowering the space or the eye.

Autumnal shades of chocolate, mustard, mushroom and rose quartz make for an inviting, cosy living room.

Channel the neo-pop art movement of the eighties with a summery palette of vibrant orange, lemon yellow and baby pink. Stripes, spots and streaks add to the fun.

28

The Living Room

Let nature be your muse and use plants as colour heroes in your dining space.

30

Using colour sparingly can sometimes have the greatest impact. Something as simple as a tangerine chair can elevate the look and feel of a room.

Shades of marsala and clay are offset by the careful placement of indoor greenery in the form of a house plant.

Warm up your living room with Mediterranean shades of coral, salmon and terracotta. Try highlighting key areas like doors and architraves (left) or go all in, painting the skirting boards the same colour as the walls for floor-to-ceiling flow (above).

Everyday objects can add colour too. This bright red ladder becomes a work of art against the solid yellow of the wall.

Give your living room a seventies feel with bright and cheery citrus tones of orange and lime green.

For a sophisticated look, try working with a combination of low-key hues like basil, olive and sandstone.

A carefully curated hotchpotch of art and objects of beauty can transcend clutter, especially in a small space, where a riot of clashing colours has an even bigger impact.

Bring the serenity of the forest into your living room with leafy plants and mossy velvets (left) or the colours of the canopy (above).

48

Seafoam, aquamarine and bottle green evoke the colours of sea glass washed ashore after a storm.

50

Brightly coloured bookshelves are a nifty, functional way to add colour to your living room without having to paint any walls.

Royal blue is a timeless hue, well suited to a classic living room look when paired with furniture in tan, taupe or caramel tones.

A dark-hued feature wall is a real standout when illuminated by streams of natural light.

Create a cosy sanctuary with rich, deep colours (above) or achieve the opposite effect – a sense of light and space – with darker halls and doorways leading into bright, airy rooms (right).

Shades of black, charcoal and gunmetal grey create a shadowy effect.

The Kitchen

A functional, utilitarian room that is often left unadorned, the kitchen is every bit as worthy of colour as other spaces in your home. That tired old splashback is the perfect place to showcase boutique tiles in porcelain or ceramic, laid out in solid blocks of colour or pleasing patterns – but that's only one of the many ways to give your kitchen a colour lift. Don your overalls and paint your cabinetry a rich burgundy, or replace your drawer handles with luxe, Art Deco-style fixtures in shining gold. Whatever you invest in brightening up your kitchen will come back to you in the form of a beautiful space to bake, brew coffee, pour wine, pack lunches and break bread.

Dusky pinks might be an unusual choice for a kitchen, but they add a touch of softness to a room that is often considered the heart of the home.

64

The Kitchen

Evoke eighties California with pops of pastel pink and baby blue in your kitchen.

Upgrading to a brand-new retro-style fridge in an eye-catching shade like fire-engine red is a quick, easy way to add a surge of colour to your kitchen. No paint or brushes required!

Create a common thread that ties your kitchen together by matching the colours of large appliances (like the fridge) to the furniture and fixtures (like stools, tapware and light fittings).

Duck-egg blue is a classic kitchen favourite. Use it to paint a corner feature wall (left) or add it to your kitchen backsplash (above).

When it comes to adding personality to your home, nothing says it like neon.

Painting your cabinets in evocative colours like lush forest green, sage or warm terracotta can transform what might otherwise be a somewhat sterile space, making your kitchen feel welcoming.

Whether you go for a brilliant peacock or understated powder blue, cool tones give your kitchen a touch of class.

Mixing and matching intricate tiles allows you to incorporate a range of colours and patterns into your kitchen.

Bold patterns and colours coexist harmoniously in kitchens where the cabinetry and countertops follow simple, clean lines.

Honour your cultural heritage or favourite holiday destination by adorning your kitchen with elaborate, decorative tiles from afar.

Recessed lighting is a subtle way to bring out the colours of a kitchen splashback, whether it be classic white subway tiles with dark grouting (left) or glossy, sunset-orange acrylic (above).

Offset dark backgrounds with neutral surfaces and a single colourful detail that draws the eye.

Create a moody, atmospheric kitchen with dark wood cabinets, a silvery-grey splashback and a stark, white countertop to balance it all out.

The Bedroom

If there's one room in your house that deserves a personal touch, it's the bedroom. Your bedroom is your sanctuary – not just where you sleep, but a place to retreat from the world, to rest, relax and daydream – and an expression of who you are. Some of us sleep best in a soft, serene space painted in calming colours, but if a phantasmagorical fever dream is more your vibe, go all out with a riot of colour – there are no rules! For a big change, apply wallpaper, paint all the walls or invest in new carpet – or for a less dramatic transition, try a new bedspread or rug. Whatever you choose to do, trust your instincts, and your dream bedroom will be a genuine reflection of you.

Mix soft pastels with earthy tones to create an ethereal, dreamy space. Use accessories like vases and cushions to elevate the room without having to paint or buy new furniture.

Decorative wallpaper can transform a tired wardrobe in an instant. A lively floral print adds a touch of natural whimsy to this room.

Go the extra mile by painting the inside of your wardrobe. Every time you open the doors, you'll be glad you did.

Add layers of colour with an ever-changing collection of bespoke textiles and curios.

101

The Bedroom

Bright white woodwork and crisp white sheets provide a pleasing contrast to the intense, glowing green of the feature wall and heavy blanket.

Offset a dark feature wall by furnishing your bedroom with softer colours, like the pale orchid, bone and chestnut used here.

Burnt-orange and olive-green hues bring a retro vibe to this bedroom, while a textured black rug grounds the space.

Exposed wooden beams contrast well with this room's whitewashed walls, pale fabrics and bold black-and-white geometric rug.

Earthy tones have a restful effect, as this room's simple wooden bedframe and ochre-coloured curtains show.

Brightly painted vintage finds and souvenirs from your travels can pack a powerful punch without a big investment of time or money.

Brighten your bedroom by adding multicoloured stripes to the space with a bedspread (left) or statement art piece (above).

Play around with colour by painting a DIY rainbow featuring your favourite shades to create the perfect space for daydreaming.

A canopy in a striking shade is a clever way to add colour and whimsy to a child's bedroom.

115

The Bedroom

Colour-blocking warm tones can create an inviting, cocoon-like retreat from the world.

Layering different patterns and textures adds interest as well as colour and life to a room.

126

Indoor plants are a natural way to add colour to the bedroom without the need for paint. Add green furnishings, bedding, artwork or accessories to multiply the effect.

To draw the eye to the view through a feature window, paint the walls and ceiling as dark as you dare to.

129

The Bedroom

The Bathroom

It doesn't matter if you're in and out of the shower in three minutes flat or love a good, long soak in the tub, bringing colour into your bathroom will elevate your everyday routine, making bathing a daily pleasure you'll look forward to. Replacing old, worn tiles is one of the most common ways to change the entire vibe of the space. Try butter yellow for a retro look, azure to evoke an island paradise, or a multihued, one-of-a-kind mosaic. For a quick and easy change, upgrade your plain, functional tapware and fixtures to glam gold, or add a touch of personality with moisture-resistant patterned wallpaper. Whatever your choice, let your beautiful bathroom become a talking point.

Start the day with a burst of sunshine all year round by painting your cabinets vivid yellow (left), or treat yourself to a custom-made stained-glass window and bathe in colourful dappled light (above).

For a retro look, give your plain white bathtub a backdrop of playful patterned wallpaper designed especially for bathrooms.

137

Give your shower a luxe lift by installing head-turning, gold-hued tiles and fixtures.

The combination of terracotta, black and white creates a textured modern aesthetic that really stands out.

Orange and white are a natural pairing, well suited to a contemporary bathroom while giving a nod to eras gone by.

140

The Bathroom

This modern bathroom tips its hat to an ancient building material with earthy, clay-coloured tiles. Matte gold fixtures add a touch of contemporary class.

Take a step back and make colour choices that change the look of the room from different viewpoints.

Playing with shapes like squares, circles or a beehive-inspired hexagon is a great way to add texture to a colour.

Let the floor under your feet do the work for you by investing in multihued terrazzo tiles with some serious wow factor (above), or go for polished, tinted concrete in the colour of your choice (right).

A statement splashback in terrazzo is a subtle way to add colour to any bathroom – classic or contemporary.

Above all, colour is versatile. Use it extravagantly, for a masterclass in maximalism (left), or judiciously, to add interest to a compact space (above).

Recreate the fresh, bracing feel of an ocean dip with bold blues in stormy Atlantic or bright Pacific hues.

The sophisticated minimalism of architectural slabs of emerald marble and slate-grey tiles evokes an ancient Japanese bathhouse.

159

The Bathroom

The high-contrast colour combo of black and white is a classic bathroom look that never goes out of style.

165

The Bathroom

The Outdoors

Whether you have a sun-drenched rooftop garden, shaded terrace, compact courtyard or petite balcony, a home's outdoor spaces always benefit from a dash of colour. While homeowners can pull off blockbuster colour makeovers to the exterior of their homes, renters can introduce a kaleidoscope of colours in other, less permanent ways by accessorising with vivid plant pots and bright outdoor furniture. Take inspiration from places around the globe that embrace the open-air lifestyle. Al fresco dining with your family and garden parties with friends are all the better with a cinematic backdrop: a stunning feature wall, vibrantly painted brickwork or perhaps a garden bed of pretty flowers in full bloom. If there is one place to let your creativity run wild, it's your home's outdoor spaces.

168

Boost the kerb appeal of your home with cute pastel shades that cast a summer glow all year round.

171

Undulating curves overlaid with soft blush tones contrast beautifully with a bright blue sky.

The Outdoors

Apply colour in an artistic way that creates a new look from every angle.

175

The Outdoors

176

This magenta wall makes a striking backdrop for a collection of plants, potted in old cans painted in a range of eye-popping colours including teal, lilac and cobalt.

It's the bubble-gum pink behind the plain white tiles, black-and-white furnishings and simple wooden shelving that makes this space look so chic.

178

The Outdoors

Make a big, bold monochromatic statement by painting the exterior walls of your home in one strong colour.

180

Give old brickwork a fresh look with a pale pink makeover.

Nothing shouts 'Look at me!' like highlighter pink.

182

The Outdoors

Give your walls a new lease on life with a lick of tomato-red paint. Potted plants add interest and contrast to the scene.

Break up a bold colour scheme with snow-white trimmings to highlight your home's best assets.

185

The Outdoors

The bright blue of this door brings out the brash pink of the bougainvillea. Be mindful of the natural colours all around you and look for ways to showcase them.

Shade cloths and awnings add dimension and protection and are another great way to introduce colour to your outdoor area.

No matter how big or small, a garden can change the way your home looks and feels. Be creative and plant a range of different species, from spring blooms to evergreen succulents and palms, for colour all year round.

Climbing and creeping plants can provide natural framing for coloured doors and windows.

Make your brickwork stand out from the pack with bold, bright painted stripes (left), or, if you're building with brick, take a risk and try colour-blocking for a geometric effect (above).

198

Mimic the Memphis design movement of the eighties and nineties by mixing different colours and shapes.

Create depth by applying a variety of colours, shapes and shading to the exterior of your home.

Classic doesn't automatically mean staid or dull. As Notting Hill's famous terraces show, a new colour scheme can bring an older-style abode into the present (above), and nothing could be more cheerful than this beautiful bright yellow front door (right).

206

The Outdoors

Transform your home into a show-stopping artwork by experimenting with texture and colour.

Harper *by* Design
An imprint of HarperCollins*Publishers*

HarperCollins*Publishers*
Australia • Brazil • Canada • France • Germany • Holland • India
Italy • Japan • Mexico • New Zealand • Poland • Spain • Sweden
Switzerland • United Kingdom • United States of America

HarperCollins acknowledges the Traditional Custodians
of the land upon which we live and work, and pays respect
to Elders past and present.

First published on Gadigal Country in Australia in 2025
by HarperCollins*Publishers* Australia Pty Limited
ABN 36 009 913 517
harpercollins.com.au

Copyright © HarperCollins*Publishers* Australia Pty Limited 2025

All rights reserved. Apart from any use as permitted under the *Copyright Act 1968*, no part may be reproduced, copied, scanned, stored in a retrieval system, recorded, or transmitted, in any form or by any means, without the prior written permission of the publisher. Without limiting the exclusive rights of any author, contributor, or the publisher of this publication, any unauthorised use of this publication to train generative artificial intelligence (AI) technologies is expressly prohibited. HarperCollins also exercises its rights under Article 4(3) of the Digital Single Market Directive 2019/790 and expressly reserves this publication from the text and data-mining exception.

HarperCollins*Publishers*
Macken House, 39/40 Mayor Street Upper
Dublin 1, D01 C9W8, Ireland

A catalogue record for this book is available from the National Library of Australia.

ISBN 978 1 4607 6850 1

Publisher: Mark Campbell
Publishing Director: Brigitta Doyle
Editor: Elizabeth Cowell
Writer: Jo Stewart
Designer: Mietta Yans, HarperCollins Design Studio
Front cover image by Swati B/Unsplash
Back cover image by Katarzyna Bialasiewicz/iStock
Colour reproduction by Splitting Image, Wantirna, Victoria
Printed and bound in China by RR Donnelley

8 7 6 5 4 3 2 1   25 26 27 28

PHOTOGRAPHY CREDITS

Adobe Stock: Miljan Andjelkovic, 147; Edalin, 178–179; Garden Guru, 191; rh2010, 154–155; William, 202

iStock: Andrey Abryutin, 149; Katarzyna Bialasiewicz, 16, 24, 27, 111, 139; boonsom, 188–189; Vasyl Cheipesh, 22; FollowTheFlow, 33; gmc3101, 190; hikesterson, 132; imaginima, 28–29; Arlette Lopez, 182–183; matesphoto, 10; mattjeacock, 11; Ninoon, 23, 25; Ruben Pinto, 176; Alex Potemkin, 63; Екатерина Тодорчук, 17; tulcarion, 145; UnitedPhotoStudio1, 34–35, 101; AJ Watt, 51

Pexels: Yusuf Timur Çelik, 203; Keegan Checks, 78; Ksenia Chernaya, 4, 160–161; Rachel Claire, 129, 165; cottonbro studio, 32; Ömer Gülen, 31; Amelia Hallsworth, 38; hello aesthe, 186; KoolShooters, 144; Patricia Luquet, 92; Victor Moragriega, 197; Muffin Land, 192; Ushindi Namegabe, 36; tuba, 163; Max Vakhtbovycn, 43, 69, 71, 82–83, 103, 134–135, 151

Shutterstock: brizmaker, 138; Ground Picture, 94, 95; New Africa, 96–97, 112; Pixel-Shot, 68

Stills: Svenja Blobel, 196; Matthew Genders, 59; Lewis Gregory, 15, 26, 60, 84–85, 98, 99, 148; Alberto Hernandez, 181; Zachary Hertzman, 180; Cydney Holm, 175; Nick Katkov, 110; Sian Fay Kerr, 37; Rebecca Newman, 204; Kenvaze Sidhu, 185; Ollie Tomlinson, 8, 54–55, 56, 127; Igor Zacharov, 172–173

Stocksy: Raymond Forbes LLC, 108; Minette Hand, 123, 126; Lumina, 115; Rowena Naylor, 121; Nibuya Qubik, 122, 137, 140–141; David Prado, 198; Katarina Radovic, 168; James Tarry, 113

Unsplash: Erol Ahmed, 169; Jahanzeb Ahsan, 206; Nima Aksoy, 117; Alexey Aladashvili, 159; Lisa Anna, 62, 136; Decima Athens, 76–77; Swati B, 18–19, 170; Sumaid pal Singh Bakshi, 21, 41; Bence Balla-Schottner, 157; Beazy, 87, 102; Lennon Cheng, 187; Collov Home Design, 47; Chastity Cortijo, 150; Curology, 6; Andrea Davis, 73; Yevhenii Deshko, 46; Juan Domenech, 171; Fatih, 166; Viktor Forgacs, 200–201; Taylor Friehl, 86; Romain Galoché, 124–125; Max Harlynking, 104–105; Sirius Harrison, 2; Josh Hemsley, 109; Kam Idris, 74, 89; Grace Kelly, 130; Dmitry Kovalchuk, 75; Jason Leung, 194; David Libeert, 30; Andrej Lišakov, 48; Lotus Design N Print, 81; Aleksandr Lyaptsev, 142; Christian Mackie, 90–91; Huy Nguyen, 118–119; Claryn Nicholas, 162; Dzordzoe Noamesi, 152; Sanju Pandita, 66–67; Eugenia Pankiv, 64; Huy Phan, 79; Prydumano Design, 107; Jamie Quirke, 12–13; Avi Richards, 106; Allison Saeng, 146; Vidisha Sanghvi, 50; sara.illustration, 205; Alex Shuper, 14, 40; Spacejoy, 44–45, 49, 70; Annie Spratt, 120; Stefen Tan, 177; Tile Merchant Ireland, 153; Umanoide, 133; Faisal Waheed, 80; Emily Wang, 52–53; Austin Wehrwein, 57; Steph Wilson, 42; Evan Wise, 116; Allen Y, 199; Te Lun Ou Yang, 195; Sam Yink, 156